WORLD WINDOWS

Land and Water

WORKBOOK

HEINLE
CENGAGE Learning™

Y|S|G
A YBM COMPANY
Young & Son
Global, Inc.

Building Background

🔴 **Read and check ✔.**

Which of the following are landforms?

Vocabulary Preview

🔴 **Match, trace, and read.**

1.  •   •  ocean

2.  •   •  hill

3.  •   •  mountain

4.  •   •  plain

5.  •   •  lake

6.  •   •  river

Vocabulary

🔴 **Look, read, and write.**

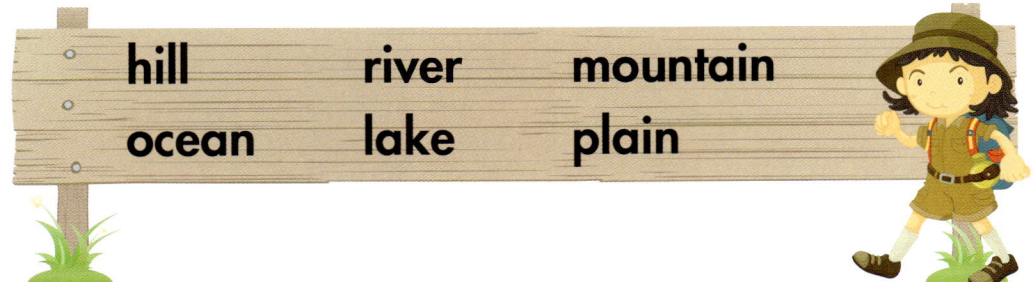

hill   river   mountain

ocean   lake   plain

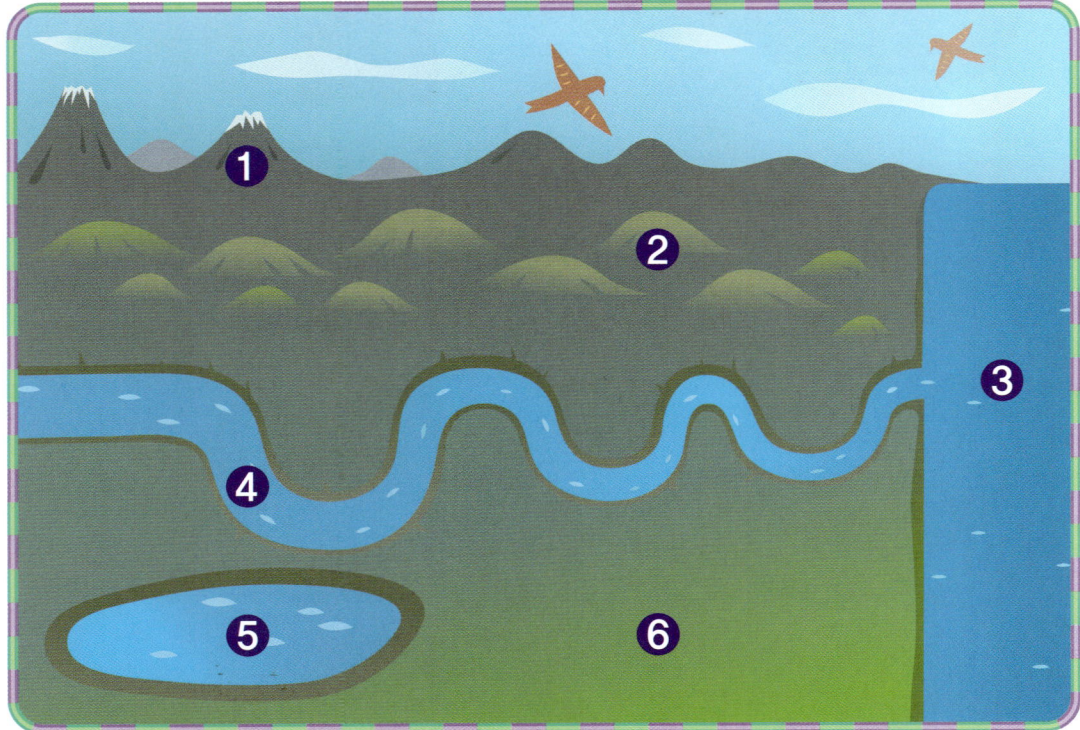

1. _____   2. _____   3. _____

4. _____   5. _____   6. _____

Read and circle.

1. A plain is a large, flat area of land.

a.  b.

2. A lake is a body of water that has land on all sides.

a.  b.

3. An ocean is the largest body of water.

a.  b.

Key Sentence 2

🔴 **Read and write.**

hill	Earth	long	fresh water
higher	mountains	water	land

1.

There are different kinds of landforms and bodies of _____ on _____.

2.

A _____ is land that is _____ than the land around it.

3.

_____ are the highest kind of _____ on Earth.

4.

A river is a _____ body of _____.

A **Read and circle.**

1. This book is about the features of _____.

   a. fresh water and salt water
   b. landforms and bodies of water

2. Plains are often _____.

   a. rocky
   b. grassy

3. Most hills have _____ tops.

   a. round
   b. steep

B **Read and write _L_ for _lakes_, _R_ for _rivers_, or _O_ for _oceans_. Some have more than one answer.**

1. _____ They are bodies of water.

2. _____ They carry water across the land.

3. _____ They have fresh water.

4. _____ They cover most of the Earth.

5. _____ They have land on all sides.

Reading Comprehension 2

🔴 **Read and circle.**

1. Some plains are good for farming.　　**True**　**False**

2. Mountains are often steep and rocky.　　**True**　**False**

3. A lake is the largest body of water on Earth.　　**True**　**False**

4. Oceans carry water across the land.　　**True**　**False**

5. The Earth's surface is different from place to place.　　**True**　**False**

A **Read and circle.**

1. What are oceans made of?

   a. Fresh water

   b. Salt water

2. Which landform has a round top?

   a. A hill

   b. A plain

3. Which body of water has land on all sides?

   a. A lake

   b. A river

B **Read and write.**

What is the highest kind of land on Earth?

_____

_____

Listening Comprehension

🔴 **Look, listen, and circle.**  7

1.

    a.   b.

2.

    a.   b.

3.

    a.   b.

4.

    a.   b.

5.

    a.   b.

6.

    a.   b.

7.

    a.   b.

8.

    a.   b.

🔴 **Listen, read, and write.**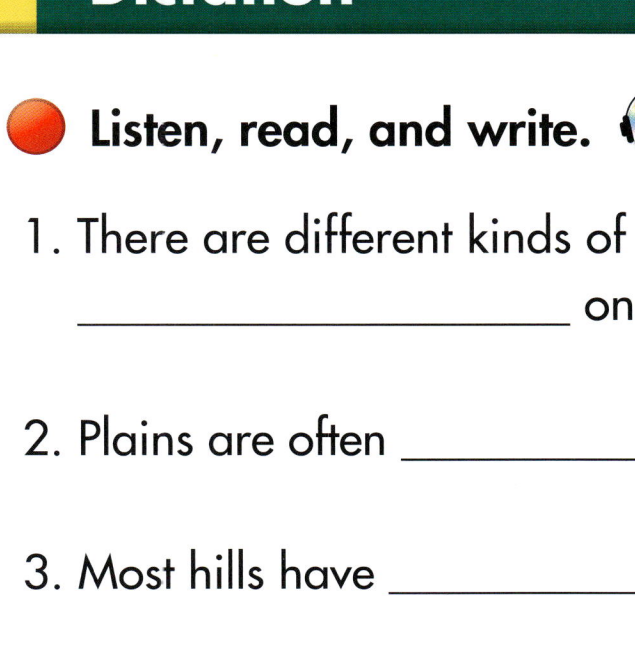

1. There are different kinds of landforms and
   _____ on Earth.

2. Plains are often _____.

3. Most hills have _____.

4. Mountains are much _____ than hills.

5. Most _____ have fresh water.

6. Rivers _____ lakes, other rivers, or oceans.

7. Oceans _____ most of the Earth.

flow into	higher	grassy	cover
round tops	lakes	bodies of water	

Grammar

🔴 **Read, circle, and write.**

1. A plain _____ a large, flat area of land.
   a. is   b. are

2. Plains _____ often grassy.
   a. is   b. are

3. Oceans _____ made of salt water.
   a. is   b. are

4. An ocean _____ the largest body of water.
   a. is   b. are

5. Mountains _____ often steep and rocky.
   a. is   b. are

● **Read and unscramble.**

1.

the highest kind of land   are

on Earth   mountains

_____

_____ .

2.

lakes, other rivers,   rivers

or oceans   flow into

_____

_____ .

3.

is different   from place

the Earth's surface   to place

_____

_____ .

Reread "Land and Water" and write.

Main Idea

There are different kinds of landforms and bodies of water on Earth.

land

water

Detail 1

A(n) _____ is a large, flat area of land.

Detail 4

A(n) _____ is a body of water that has land on all sides.

Detail 2

A(n) _____ is land that is higher than the land around it.

Detail 5

A(n) _____ is a long body of water.

Detail 3

A mountain is the _____ kind of land on Earth.

Detail 6

A(n) _____ is the largest body of water.

lake   highest   ocean   plain   river   hill

lake	hill
ocean	mountain
river	plain